MOVIE SONGS

By Special Arrangement

Alto Saxophone

Eleve
A
CAR

GW00646612

Jazz-Style Arrangements
With a "Variation"

CONTENTS

Project Manager/Editor: Thom Proctor
Production Coordinator: Karl Bork
Art Design: Thais Yanes
Engraver: Mark Burgess
CD Producer: Teena Chinn
Recording Engineer: Kendall Thomsen
Recorded at Starke Lake Studios

Flute, Clarinet, Alto Sax, Tenor Sax: Jeff Rupert
Trumpet: Tom Macklin
F Horn: Kathy Gabriel
Trombone: Jeff Thomas
Piano and Keyboards: Teena Chinn
Guitar: Lindsay Blair
Bass: Charles Archard
Drums and Percussion: Keith Wilson

WARNER BROS. PUBLICATIONS
Warner Music Group
An AOL Time Warner Company
USA: 15800 NW 48th Avenue, Miami, FL 33014

IMP
INTERNATIONAL MUSIC PUBLICATIONS LIMITED
ENGLAND: GRIFFIN HOUSE,
161 HAMMERSMITH ROAD, LONDON W6 8BS

ALTO SAXOPHONE

SWEET GEORGIA BROWN

Words and Music by
BEN BERNIE, MACEO PINKARD
and KENNETH CASEY
Arranged by CARL STROMMEN

0705B

OVER THE RAINBOW

Music by HAROLD ARLEN
Lyric by E.Y. HARBURG
Arranged by CARL STROMMEN

0705B

A DAY IN THE LIFE OF A FOOL

Words by CARL SIGMAN
Music by LUIZ BONFA
Arranged by CARL STROMMEN

The Simpsons

Demonstration

Backing

By Danny Elfman

Rather fast

BYE, BYE, BLACKBIRD

Words by MORT DIXON
Music by RAY HENDERSON
Arranged by CARL STROMMEN

0705B

0705B

AS TIME GOES BY

Words and Music by HERMAN HUPFELD
Arranged by CARL STROMMEN

DAYS OF WINE AND ROSES

Lyric by JOHNNY MERCER
Music by HENRY MANCINI
Arranged by CARL STROMMEN

0705B

EMILY

Music by JOHNNY MANDEL
Words by JOHNNY MERCER
Arranged by CARL STROMMEN

THE WAY YOU LOOK TONIGHT

Words by DOROTHY FIELDS
Music by JEROME KERN
Arranged by CARL STROMMEN

MISTY

Music by ERROLL GARNER
Arranged by CARL STROMMEN

ON GREEN DOLPHIN STREET

Music by BRONISLAU KAPER
Lyrics by NED WASHINGTON
Arranged by CARL STROMMEN

ALMOST LIKE BEING IN LOVE

Lyrics by ALAN JAY LERNER
Music by FREDERICK LOEWE
Arranged by CARL STROMMEN

HOW TO USE THIS BOOK

Because of the great melodies and rich chord progressions, the music from movies continues to be fertile ground for jazz players. The transcribed solos have been slightly altered to conform to a moderate degree of difficulty. The player should use the written solo section as a guide and a springboard to personal improvising efforts.

The nuances of the jazz style are impossible to notate exactly. Key to this style is the concept of the swing or syncopated rhythm. The treatment and interpretation of eighth notes largely contribute to this elusive feel. In rock or Latin style music, eighth notes are played as written, evenly, with the accent on the downbeat: ♫♫♫ ♫♫♫

Swing eight notes are treated differently at different tempos, but they are always written as even eighths. At moderate tempos the figure ♫♫♫ ♫♫♫ would be played as ♪♪♪♪♪♪ . At bright tempos, the swing feel tends to flatten out and is played more evenly with the pulse on the second half of the beat: ♫♫♫ ♫♫♫ .

Slower tempos (ballads) also tend to have a slightly more even eighth note feel. (Notice in listening to some solos that although the rhythm section is playing in a 12/8 feel, the solo is being played with even eighth notes.)

Players who are used to playing only in orchestral or wind ensemble settings have to make the adjustment of observing and interpreting eighth notes differently when placed in a big band or small group environment.

Some of the following unique jazz articulations are written out in these arrangements, but you can add more, tastefully, to create your own style.

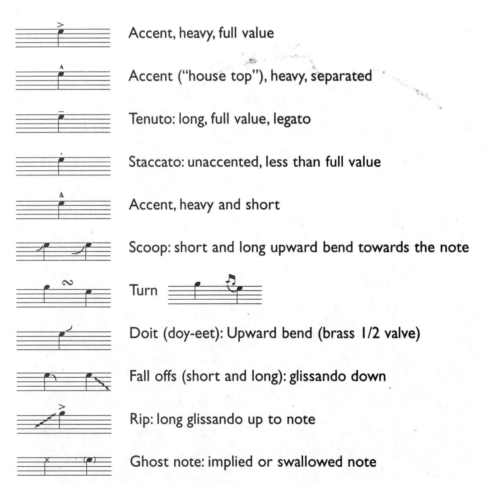

Accent, heavy, full value

Accent ("house top"), heavy, separated

Tenuto: long, full value, legato

Staccato: unaccented, less than full value

Accent, heavy and short

Scoop: short and long upward bend towards the note

Turn

Doit (doy-eet): Upward bend (brass 1/2 valve)

Fall offs (short and long): glissando down

Rip: long glissando up to note

Ghost note: implied or swallowed note

Also available: *Gershwin® By Special Arrangement* and *Broadway By Special Arrangement*, arranged by Carl Strommen.

For more information and further study of improvisation, refer to the Jazz Improvisation Series books *Approaching the Standards* by Dr. Willie L. Hill, Jr., published by Warner Bros. Publications.